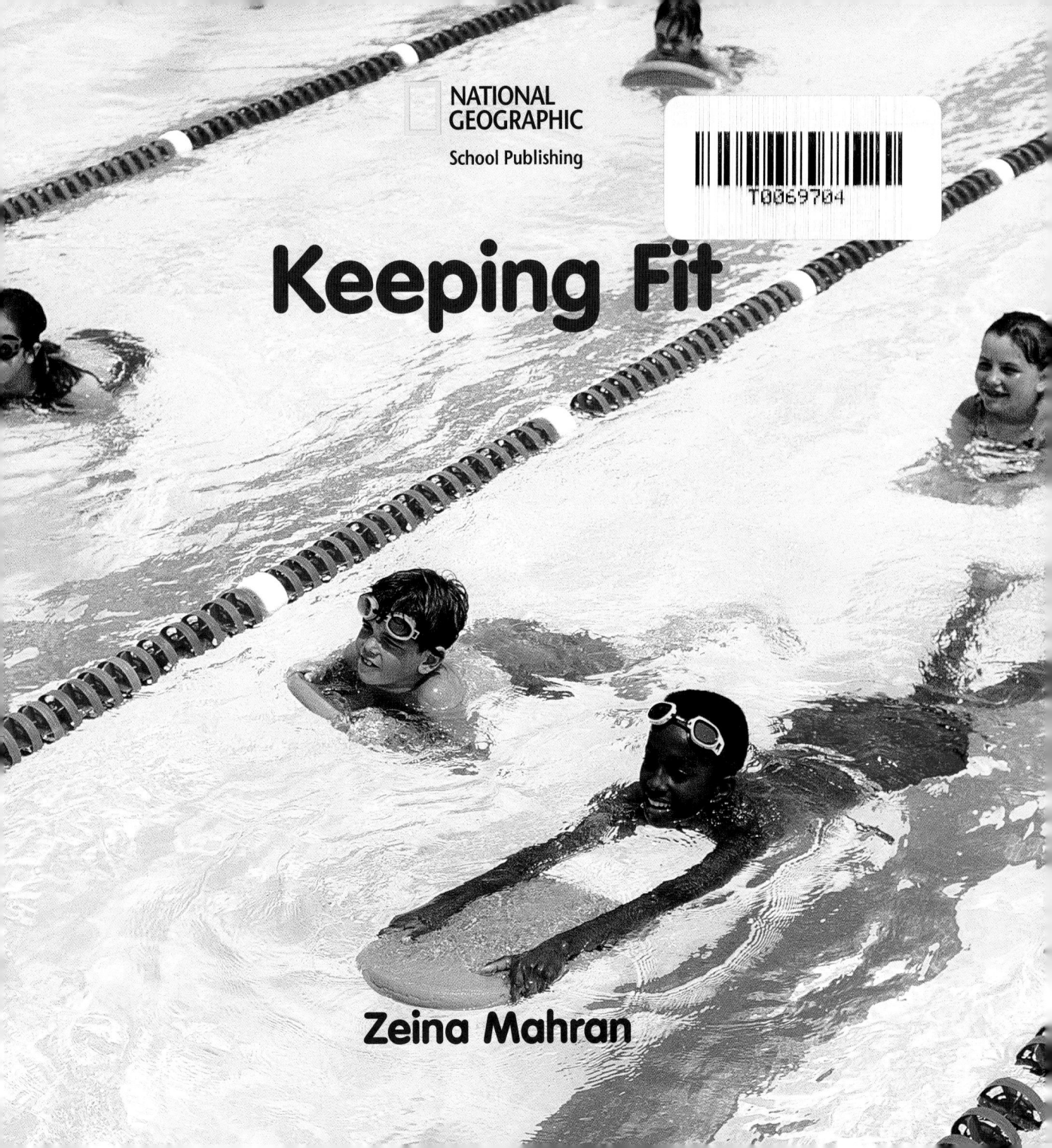

NATIONAL GEOGRAPHIC
School Publishing

T0069704

Keeping Fit

Zeina Mahran

PICTURE CREDITS
Illustration by Ivan Finnegan (14–15).
Cover, 1, 2, 4 (all), 5 (above right), 6, 7 (left), 8, 9 (all), 10 (right), 11 (below), 13 (all), 14 (center), 15 (center & below), Photolibrary.com; 5 (left), 7 (right), 10 (left), 11 (above right), 12, 15 (above), Getty Images; 5 (below right), 14 (above & below), APL/Corbis.

Produced through the worldwide resources of the National Geographic Society, John M. Fahey, Jr., President and Chief Executive Officer; Gilbert M. Grosvenor, Chairman of the Board; Nina D. Hoffman, Executive Vice President and President, Books and Education Publishing Group.

PREPARED BY NATIONAL GEOGRAPHIC SCHOOL PUBLISHING
Ericka Markman, Senior Vice President and President Children's Books and Education Publishing Group; Steve Mico, Senior Vice President and Publisher; Marianne Hiland, Editorial Director; Lynnette Brent, Executive Editor; Michael Murphy and Barbara Wood, Senior Editors; Bea Jackson, Design Director; David Dumo, Art Director; Margaret Sidlowsky, Illustrations Director; Matt Wascavage, Manager of Publishing Services; Sean Philpotts, Production Manager.

MANUFACTURING AND QUALITY MANAGEMENT
Christopher A. Liedel, Chief Financial Officer; Phillip L. Schlosser, Director; Clifton M. Brown III, Manager.

BOOK DEVELOPMENT
Ibis for Kids Australia Pty Limited.

Copyright © 2006 National Geographic Society. All rights reserved. Reproduction of the whole or any part of the contents without written permission from the publisher is prohibited. National Geographic, National Geographic *Windows on Literacy*, and the Yellow Border are registered trademarks of the National Geographic Society.

Published by the National Geographic Society
1145 17th Street, N.W.
Washington, D.C. 20036-4688

ISBN-13: 978-0-7922-6069-1
ISBN-10: 0-7922-6069-4

6 7 19 18
Printed in USA

Contents

Think and Discuss	4
Fit and Healthy	6
Fun and Games	8
Everyday Activities	10
Energy for Exercise	12
Use What You Learned	14
Picture Glossary	16

walk
swim

run
play
ride a bike

Fit and Healthy

Exercise helps you keep fit and healthy. There are many ways to exercise.

swim
skate

Fun and Games

There are fun ways to exercise.
You exercise when you play active games.

jump rope

play hopscotch
play soccer

Everyday Activities

You can exercise when you do everyday activities.

climb stairs
walk a dog
TAURUS

Energy for Exercise

You need energy to exercise.
Eating healthy food gives you energy.

Sleep gives you energy, too.

Green Park

exercise

fun

game

healthy

keep fit

park

play

run

walk

Picture Glossary

basketball

eat

hopscotch

play

skate

sleep

soccer

swim